DATE DUE

JAN - 2 2001	
AUG 2 8 2001	
NOV 0 3 2001	
DEC 1 2 2001	
MAR 7 - 2003	
JUN 1 0 2006	
DEC 1 6 2007	

DEMCO, INC. 38-2931

Amazing Science Experiments with Everyday Materials

E. Richard Churchill
Illustrated by Frances Zweifel

Sterling Publishing Co., Inc.   New York

Library of Congress Cataloging-in-Publication Data

Churchill, E. Richard (Elmer Richard)
    Amazing science experiments with everyday materials / E. Richard
Churchill : illustrated by Frances Zweifel.
        p.   cm.
    Includes index.
    Summary: More than sixty simple physics experiments that can
safely be done with materials around the house.
    ISBN 0-8069-7372-2
    1. Science—Experiments—Juvenile literature. [1. Science—
Experiments.   2. Experiments.]   I. Zweifel, Frances W., ill.
II. Title.
Q164.C46   1991
530'.078—dc20   90-20641
                                                            CIP
                                                            AC

10 9 8 7 6 5 4 3 2 1

Text © 1991 by E. Richard Churchill
Illustrations © 1991 by Sterling Publishing Company, Inc.
Published by Sterling Publishing Company, Inc.
387 Park Avenue South, New York, N.Y. 10016
Distributed in Canada by Sterling Publishing
% Canadian Manda Group, P.O. Box 920, Station U
Toronto, Ontario, Canada M8Z 5P9
Distributed in Great Britain and Europe by Cassell PLC
Villiers House, 41/47 Strand, London WC2N 5JE, England
Distributed in Australia by Capricorn Ltd.
P.O. Box 665, Lane Cove, NSW 2066
Manufactured in the United States of America

Sterling ISBN 0-8069-7372-2 Trade

For Chum
with love and
other warm thoughts

Contents

Before You Begin

Science experiments aren't just for scientists and college students. They are fun for everybody—that includes you and me. What's even better, the experiments in this book all have a little surprise in them. Some of them surprise you because they work. Others are surprising because of what happens.

You won't have to look for lots of hard-to-find materials in order to do these experiments. Everything you need to carry them out can usually be found right around the house.

Also, you won't have to spend your money on chemicals and test tubes and other scientific equipment in order to have fun with these projects. They won't cost you a thing.

And, you don't have to worry about blowing yourself up. The worst that these experiments will do is crack you up. They are great fun for entertaining others as well as yourself.

All the experiments in this book work. We tested each and every one to make sure. If one doesn't seem to work, just reread the instructions and give it another go. When you get everything just right, the experiment will work. That's a promise!

You may decide that some of these experiments are really stunts or tricks. That's true. It is also true that lots of the best stunts and tricks work because they are based on scientific principles. This book just helps you put science to work in ways that may seem impossible, but which are always fun and entertaining.

Happy experimenting!

SLOW START—FAST FINISH

You know how you feel when you're lying in bed in the morning and you don't want to move? That's inertia.

You're on your bike at the foot of a steep hill and it takes every ounce of strength you have just to get the bike started. That, too, is inertia.

Inertia is a scientific word that says that things that are standing still tend to continue to stand still.

When you are riding your bike along a level road, you don't have to pedal hard every second. In fact, you can stop spinning the pedals and coast a bit. That's inertia.

You see, inertia also means that objects that are moving tend to keep on moving.

These ideas aren't hard to understand. Of course things stand still until someone or something moves them. What would life be like if you put a pizza on a table and, all by itself, it started to slide to the edge and fall onto the floor?

Engineers found out long ago that the family car uses only a small part of its power to cruise along the highway. It takes much greater horsepower to get that car moving and up to speed than to keep it going once it's on the open road.

The experiments we're going to do in this chapter show how you can make inertia work for you. Some of the results will amaze you and your friends. If you wish, let them think you're performing a bit of magic.

The Amazing Bottom Checker

Can you remove the bottom checker in a stack without touching the other checkers in the stack and without having the stack tip over?

You need:
9–11 checkers (or a small stack of coins)

What to do:
Build a stack of eight or ten checkers. If you use coins, make sure they are all the same size. Medium-sized coins are best.

Place another checker beside the stack. Leave about an inch between this checker and the stack.

Flip the single checker hard with your forefinger or your middle finger. Give it a really hard snap.

What happens:
The bottom checker will fly out from the stack. If all goes well, the rest will stay neatly in place.

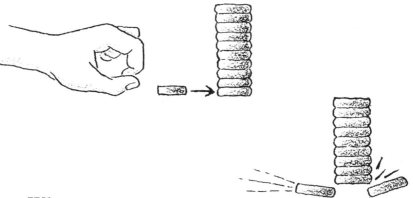

Why:
Inertia keeps the stack of checkers from moving even when the bottom one is suddenly snapped away. Because the stack was not moving to start

with it tends to stay that way. Scientists say, "A body at rest tends to remain at rest."

What now:
To vary this experiment, you need a pencil. Use it to hit one of the checkers in the middle of the stack. Hit it sharply and be sure to hit only one. With a bit of practice you can knock any checker out of the stack without tipping the stack over.

Catching Coins on Your Elbow

Here's a great trick that is also a neat science experiment.

You need:
4–5 coins
   or checkers

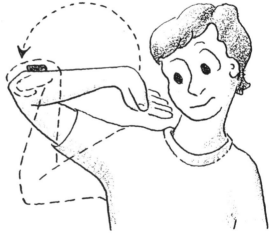

What to do:
Place one coin or checker on your elbow.

Hold your arm parallel to the floor or the coin will fall off.

You are now going to catch the coin that is on your elbow. That wouldn't be much of a trick except for one thing. You are going to catch it in the same hand whose elbow is now holding the coin.

Here's how it works. In one sudden, very quick move you will drop your arm. This causes your open hand to snap forward. The arrow in the drawing shows the direction your hand will move.

At the same time your elbow will fall away from under the coin.

What happens:

As your elbow moves from under the coin your hand will come down from it. Once you get your timing down, you'll catch the coin every time.

Why:

Since the coin is still it tends to remain in that position. Good old inertia again! When your elbow moves rapidly it just drops out from under the coin. This leaves the coin hanging in air. Gravity pulls the coin towards the ground, but inertia gives it a slow start. Your hand is faster than the coin because your hand is already moving.

What now:

Once you have the hang of it, add a second coin on top of the first, and then three or four or more and catch them all at once.

What a Crazy Way to Break Thread

You can cut thread or even break it between your hands. Here's a way to break a piece of thread you never thought of!

You need:

a hammer or other unbreakable object that weighs about 2 pounds (1 kg)

3 feet (1 m) of cotton thread
a short string
scissors

What to do:

Choose a hammer or other object that won't break if it is dropped. A heavy wrench or a chunk of wood will work just fine. Go outside to perform this experiment.

Tie a loop of string around the hammer like this:

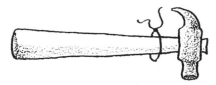

Next, cut the sewing thread in half. Be sure to use cotton thread because nylon won't work.

Tie the end of one piece of thread to the top of the string loop. Then tie the second piece of thread to the bottom of the loop, like this:

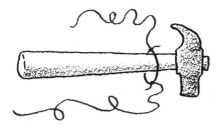

Tie the loose end of the top thread to something solid so the hammer hangs below it. A tree branch is great but any strong support will work fine.

Make sure there is nothing you can break or hurt beneath the hammer.

Once you set up the experiment, get a firm grip on the bottom string. The arrow shows where to grab. Then give a sudden, hard jerk downwards.

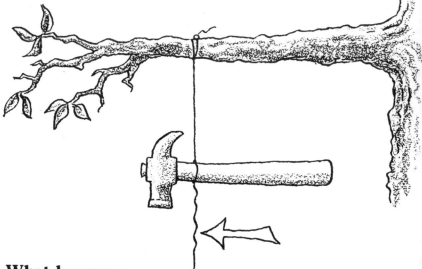

What happens:

You're expecting the hammer to fall on your hand, aren't you? What happens is the thread breaks somewhere between your hand and the hammer. The hammer will continue to hang from the top thread.

Why:

Even though the hammer doesn't weigh much, it takes a lot of energy to get it moving when it is at rest. The sudden downward pull causes the thread to break because it is not strong enough to over-come the inertia of the hammer.

That's a Lot of Work to Put Soap in a Glass

This experiment in inertia is impressive even if there's no good reason to put a bar of soap in a glass.

You need:

a large drinking glass
a plastic plate or the
   side from a cereal
   box
tape or glue

an empty matchbox
   or a piece of cereal
   box
a small bar of soap

What to do:

Set the glass on the table with its rim up. (Don't use the family's best crystal, please.)

Place a plastic plate like the ones from frozen foods on top of the glass. If you don't have a plastic plate use an eight-inch (20 cm) piece square of cardboard—it could also be round, if you want.

Next set the outside of a small matchbox on top of the plate. If you don't have a matchbox, you can make one. Take a look at the instructions on page 16.

Set the bar of soap on the matchbox. The drawing shows how.

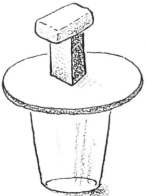

Get a firm grip on the glass with one hand.

Strike the edge of the plate or cardboard with your other hand. Make the blow hard and fast.

What happens:

The plate flies into the air (so be sure there's nothing breakable near it). The soap holder tumbles off and the soap plops into the glass.

Why:

Inertia strikes again!

MAKING A MATCHBOX

Cut a piece of cereal box material 2½ inches by 5 inches (6 cm × 12 cm). Fold it along each dotted line as shown below. Fasten the overlapping end with tape or glue.

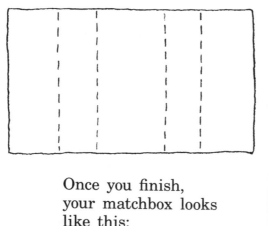

Once you finish, your matchbox looks like this:

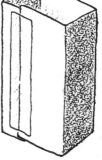

Watching Inertia at Work

Here's a simple experiment that lets you see inertia at work.

You need:

four feet (1 m) of string

a rubber band
a book or brick

What to do:

Tie the string around the book or brick. Then tie the free end of the string to the rubber band.

Set the book or brick on the floor. Rough carpet is best. Just don't use a polished floor that a brick might scratch. Things look like this now:

Pull on the rubber band.

What happens:

The rubber band will stretch until you get the load moving. Then, as you continue to pull the weight across the floor, the rubber band won't stretch quite so much as when you started pulling.

Why:

Inertia tends to keep motionless things where they are. In order to get things moving, you have to overcome inertia. The greater stretch in the rubber band shows you had to pull harder to get the load started than you have to pull to keep it moving after that.

The Strange Case of the Marble in the Bottle

Anyone can drop a marble or a coin into a bottle. But can it be done without touching the marble?

You need:
an empty bottle
a sheet of cereal box material

scissors
a marble, coin or checker

What to do:
Make sure the open mouth of the bottle is larger than the marble, coin, or checker you are going to drop into it.

Cut a piece of cereal box material about four inches by four inches (10 cm × 10 cm). Place it on top of the bottle. Place the marble or coin or checker on the cardboard so it is right over the bottle's mouth. (It's a good idea to hold off on using a marble until you see how this all works. A coin or checker is easier to handle.)

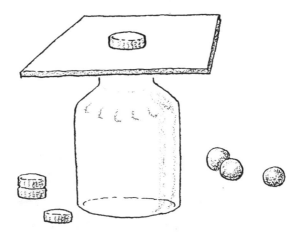

Flip the edge of the card hard and fast with your finger. If you're thinking like a scientist, you'll remember how you flipped one checker into another to knock the bottom checker out of the stack.

What happens:
The card snaps out from between the marble and the bottle. The marble drops into the bottle without your touching it. Pretty neat!

Why:
The marble is standing still. Inertia wants to keep it that way. The card snaps away so quickly that the marble has no chance to follow the card. Gravity pulls it down into the bottle.

If the card moves too slowly, the marble will follow the card instead of falling into the bottle.

What now:
If you want to get fancy, try this with two marbles!

Slow But Steady

Here's an experiment you'll be able to perform only if you're willing to go about it slowly and with a steady hand.

You need:

scissors
a sheet of paper
a pencil

a bottle with a small
mouth and neck

What to do:

Cut a strip of paper three inches wide and ten or eleven inches long (7 cm × 25 cm).

Place the bottle upside down on the paper near the edge of a table like this:

Your goal is to remove the paper without tipping the bottle over.

Place the pencil on the loose end of the paper and carefully roll the paper around the pencil. Keep rolling very slowly until the rolled paper touches the mouth of the bottle. Then, with a steady hand continue rolling the paper.

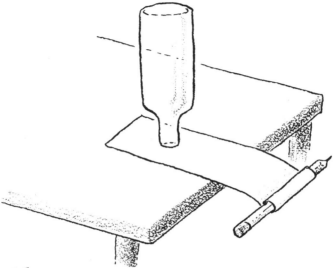

What happens:
As you slowly and steadily keep rolling, the paper gradually creeps out from under the bottle, which won't tip over.

Why:
The unmoving bottle tends to stay motionless and upright because of inertia. The bottle's mouth can't move because it touches the rolled paper. It doesn't tip over because inertia tends to keep it exactly where it was to begin with—so long as you don't make any sudden moves.

Nail Driving the Hard Way

It's one thing to drive a nail into a board. It's another to do it holding the board in your lap.

You need:

a hammer

a wooden board (a piece of 2×4)

a thick newspaper

several nails

2 or 3 large books or a huge dictionary

What to do:

Stack the dictionary and another large book on your lap. Or use two or three large books, if you don't have a dictionary. Place a thick newspaper on top of the books to protect them.

Finish off the stack by placing the board on top of the newspaper. Any scrap of lumber will do the job. Now you are going to pound a nail into the board. That's right. You'll pound the nail while holding the board in your lap.

What happens:

As you pound the nail, you feel the force of the hammer blows on your legs, but it won't hurt.

Just make sure you don't pound the nail all the way through the board. You'll avoid this if you use a piece of 2×4. It's thick enough so that you won't find the nail going through the board before you realize it.

Why:

Inertia saves the day. The weight or mass of the books is so great, it absorbs the hammer blows without ever getting into motion.

What now:

You can experiment using fewer books. Then, for effect, let someone else hammer the nail. Just be sure you always have a thick newspaper pad between the board and the books. Also, make sure anyone swinging the hammer holds it so that the hammer head doesn't come down towards you. The hammer person needs to stand or kneel at your side and aim the hammer away from your face and body.

KEEPING YOUR BALANCE

How many times have you walked along a curb or on top of a stone wall with your arms out at your sides to help you keep your balance? Even as a tot you understood that in order to keep your balance you had to have as much weight on one side of you as on the other. You knew this instinctively.

You also discovered how easy it was to lose your balance when you walked any wall or narrow line. Instead of stepping off the wall or falling you bent and twisted and waved your arms a bit. When you did these things your body was regaining its balance by getting its center of gravity right over the curb—or whatever it was you were walking along.

Everyone knows how gravity works. Gravity is that invisible force that keeps us from flying off into space. It's the force that makes your slice of bread fall jelly-side down when you accidentally drop it. Gravity is the pull that turns your home-run into a double when the ball falls inside the park. But what is the *center* of gravity? And what does it have to do with keeping your balance?

The center of gravity is that point in an object where there is as much weight on one side as on the other. When you're walking along a curb or crack in the concrete, your center of gravity is right on the line where you place your feet. If you stand up straight with your feet spread, your center of gravity is between your feet and straight down in a line from your nose.

When we locate the center of gravity in an object we can get that object to balance. You've balanced a pencil on your finger when things got a little boring in class, haven't you? Its center of gravity is halfway from the eraser to the point—unless you have one of those big football or basketball erasers. In that case, the center of gravity is closer to the eraser than to the point.

If you want to impress people, you can refer to the center of gravity as the "point of balance." Whichever term you use, there are some really great bits of science that depend on finding where things are in balance.

The Incredible Balancing Hammer

Anyone can stand a hammer on its head and it will balance. But can you tie a hammer to a ruler and balance them both on the edge of a table with only one end of the ruler touching the table?

You need:
a hammer
a ruler

1½ feet (.5 m) of
  strong string

What to do:
Tie one end of the string around a ruler.

Tie the other end of the string around the hammer handle. Tie it tightly so it won't slip up and down the handle.

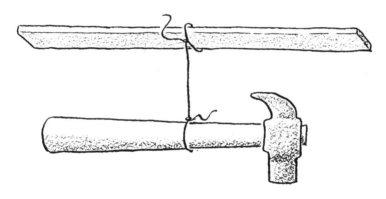

What happens:
Now to make things balance. Be sure the end of the hammer handle touches the end of the ruler. Position the ruler so that about three or four inches (10 cm) of it are on top of the table. Carefully test the ruler and hammer to see if they are in balance.

You may have to adjust the string to get the hammer to hang correctly. If you have problems

getting things to balance, shorten the string between the hammer and ruler. Don't give up if
things don't balance at first. They will once you adjust the string to the perfect length.

Why:

You positioned the hammer and ruler so that the
center of gravity is right at the edge of the table. If
you look at things from one side, you'll see that the
head of the hammer is on one side of the center of
gravity and the handle and most of the ruler are
on the other.

A hammer with a wooden handle will have a different center of gravity than one with a steel
handle because of the heavier weight of the metal
handle.

The Amazing Balancing Yardstick

It's not hard to balance a yardstick on top of your hands when you hold your hands apart. The surprising thing is how difficult it is to make that yardstick lose its balance.

You need:
a yardstick or a dowel rod

What to do:
Hold the yardstick between two outstretched fingers as shown below.

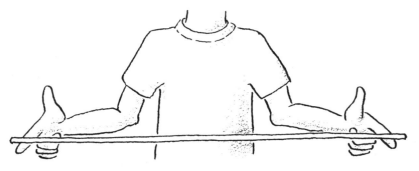

The object of this experiment is to move one finger towards the center of the yardstick until the yardstick loses its balance and tips over. Make this move slowly and steadily. It isn't fair to suddenly jerk your finger to the center of the yardstick.

What happens:
A strange thing happens as you move your finger towards the center of the yardstick. You only move one finger along the yardstick but the other finger moves along too.

Eventually you find yourself with both fingers side by side and the yardstick is still balanced.

Try it and see.

Why:
The yardstick's center of gravity is right in the middle. When you slowly move one finger towards the center of gravity the yardstick begins to tip towards that finger because that finger is nearer the center of gravity. When it tips, even slightly, it reduces the weight on the finger that isn't moving.

When less weight presses on the unmoving finger, that finger begins to slide along the yardstick. This is because there is less friction on that finger. The finger you moved first has more friction because more weight is on it. Friction slows down movement, so that less friction means faster movement.

The yardstick keeps rebalancing itself as your fingers slowly move towards one another.

The Rapid Ruler and Slowpoke Yardstick

Everyone knows that babies are likely to take a lot of tumbles when they are learning to walk. This is because they are learning how to control their bodies. Did you know that people's height has something to do with how fast they fall?

You need:
a yardstick or long dowel rod
a ruler or short dowel rod

What to do:
Begin by standing a ruler and a yardstick side by side with a few inches between them. Steady each of them with just the tip of your finger as shown in the drawing.

If you don't have a ruler and a yardstick, two dowel rods or other straight pieces of wood will work perfectly.

Lean the ruler and yardstick forward just a tiny bit to make sure both of them will fall in the same direction. Be sure they both have the same amount of forward lean. Now let go.

Why:

The center of balance for the yardstick is higher than it is for the ruler. The farther that center of balance is from the table the longer it will take the object to complete its fall.

This does not mean that a high center of gravity makes an object steadier than one with a low center of gravity. Just the opposite! Auto makers try to keep the center of gravity as low as possible so that cars are less likely to tip over. And that's why big trucks and trailers sometimes are required to pull off the highway during high winds. Not only do they have lots of surface to catch the wind but their center of gravity is high. Therefore they are more likely to turn over than are cars with a low center of gravity.

What happens:

The ruler will win the race to the ground every time. Try it and see!

What you've just seen helps explain why if a child and a taller adult start to fall forward at the same instant, the child will finish falling first. This also helps explain why babies seem to fall so fast at times.

The Mysterious Balancing Dinner Fork

Can you balance a dinner fork, a potato, and a pencil so that only the pencil's tip touches the table?

You need:

a very small potato or   a pencil
   a chunk of potato or   a fork
   a lump of modeling clay   a newspaper

What to do:

Press a long wooden pencil through the center of the potato or apple. If anyone objects to your sticking things into the family vegetables, a lump of soft modeling clay will do just as well.

Be careful doing this: Place the potato on a thick pad of newspapers. Don't hold the potato in the palm of your hand! If you do, you may run the pencil point into your hand the way I did.

Slowly and firmly push the pencil point into the potato. Once the point pokes through, pick up the potato and hold it by its sides. Carefully push the pencil on through until about 1½ inches (4 cm) or less stick out.

Once you've gotten the pencil through the potato, press the tines of the dinner fork into one side of the potato so the fork is at about the angle shown here.

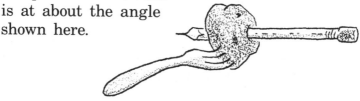

Rest the pointed end of the pencil on the edge of a table as shown below.

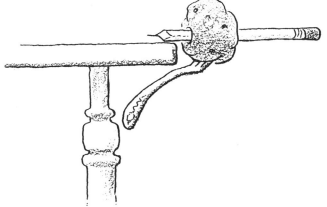

What happens:

If you're having a lucky day, the whole thing will balance right away. If it doesn't, try moving the pencil tip farther onto the table or nearer the edge.

You can also slide the potato backwards or forwards a bit along the pencil. By now this strange combination has probably balanced. If it hasn't, you can begin to feel which direction it is going to move as you steady it with your hands.

Don't give up if it doesn't balance the first few times. Keep adjusting it. If necessary, pull the fork out and replace it at a different angle.

When the combination does balance, it looks as if you have found a way to defy the laws of gravity. With a little practice, you can adjust this so that the pencil actually slopes downhill and only its point touches the table.

Why:

This is the same principle as on page 28. You must have as much weight on one side of the center of gravity as on the other.

Twice the Balancing Magic

So long as you've already messed up a potato, grab another fork and try another impossible feat of balance.

You need:

a very small potato or
    a chunk of potato or
    a lump of clay
2 forks

a pencil
a drinking glass or
    bottle and lid

What to do:

If you haven't already pulled the pencil out of the potato from the last experiment, leave it just the way it was. Otherwise, push the pencil through the potato just as carefully as you did before.

You can leave the fork in at the same angle as before if it's still sticking in the potato. Now add a second fork by pushing its tines into the side of the potato opposite the first fork. Try to stick in both forks at the same angle.

Things look
pretty much
like this:

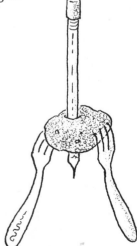

Turn a tall glass over so you can set the project on top of the glass as seen below. Instead of a glass you can use a soda pop or salad oil bottle or any bottle with a small neck and wide bottom.

What happens:

By adjusting the angle and location of the forks you can make the pencil stand straight up or lean to one side. Of course, only the point of the pencil touches the glass or top of the bottle.

It is amazing how far you can get the pencil to lean to one side if you arrange the forks in the right position.

Why:

Study the balancing figure and you'll see that there is exactly as much weight on any side of the pencil point as on any other side. The point of the pencil is the center of gravity.

HOW TO HAVE ALL THE MOVES

We already know a lot about motion. We know that many things move. We know that things that are not moving tend to remain still and stay in one place because of inertia. In order to get something to move that is standing or sitting still we have to apply some sort of force to it.

Force can be as simple as giving a toy a push to start it moving. Force can be the wind that fills a sail, carrying a boat across the lake.

Applying force to an object can be complicated, too. It may involve running an engine or motor so that a pulley can turn.

That pulley may cause a belt to go around and around, which, in turn, transfers the force to another pulley. This process can go on and become more and more complicated until, finally, a cutting device is put into motion that carefully produces a delicate part for an expensive machine.

We know that once the power of force is applied to an object, that object tends to keep on moving. Once the power or force runs out, a moving object begins to slow down and eventually stops. Gravity pulls on objects and helps to slow them down and use up their force. So does air or wind resistance. If it were not for gravity and wind resistance, you could hit a home run without having to stop and think about it.

We know that movement and motion can change with the center of gravity. By changing the center of gravity, you can turn an object or tip it over. In the last chapter we created objects that stopped moving once we located their center of gravity. Now let's deal with some other things that affect motion and the way things move.

The Turtle and the Hare

Remember the story of the turtle and the hare? When the turtle finally passes the finish line, it says something like, "Slow and steady wins the race."

You need:

2 plastic bottles exactly alike (2-liter soft drink bottles are ideal)

2 boards (or a sloping surface)

water

What to do:

Fill one of the plastic bottles half full of water. Be sure the lid is screwed on good and tight. Leave the second bottle empty.

Place the two bottles side by side at the top of a ramp or slope. A concrete sidewalk or driveway that runs downhill for a few feet and then levels out will be just fine.

You can also make a ramp from two boards of the same length. Place one end of each board on a chair and let the lower ends of the boards rest on the floor as shown in the drawing.

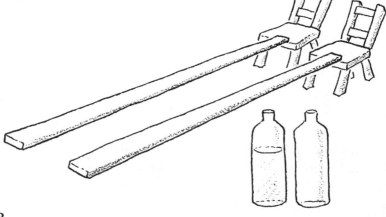

Hold the bottles at the top of the slope and then release them at the same time. Watch carefully as they roll down the slope.

What happens:
The two bottles start together. But wait! One bottle starts off faster. That's the hare in this race. However, when the bottles reach the level floor, the slower bottle (that's the turtle) rolls farther than the "hare" that took off faster.

Why:
Rub two things together and you create friction. To prove this, just rub your hands together rapidly. Feel the heat that you generate by the rubbing. Heat is created by friction.

The water in the half-filled bottle gave it extra weight. This added weight made it take off faster down the slope. However, the water rubbing against the sides of the half-filled bottle created friction. The friction slowed that bottle down.

Friction not only creates heat: it slows movement. Auto makers use oil in an automobile engine to cut down on friction and heat. They use grease to lubricate other moving parts for the same reason.

Racing Hoops

You're used to watching horses and cars race. Maybe you even watch roller skaters race. Well, here's a race the likes of which you've never seen.

You need:

2 strips of paper   scissors   ruler
    2½ × 11 inches   4 paper clips   tape
    (6 cm × 27 cm)

What to do:

For this experiment you need two paper hoops exactly the same size. (It wouldn't be fair to race hoops of different sizes against each other.)

Cut two strips of notebook paper as long as the sheet of paper and 2½ inches (6 cm) wide. Make each strip into a hoop by taping or gluing the narrow ends together.

Now tape a paper clip inside one of the two hoops like this:

Be sure the paper
clip is in the exact
center of the hoop.

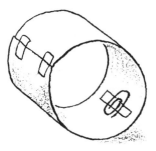

Place the two hoops side by side a few inches apart at the top of a slope or ramp. (The ramp you used for the turtle and hare race is perfect.)

Let go of the hoops at the same time. (If there is much of a breeze blowing, by the way, you'll need to use an indoor ramp.)

What happens:

If you look closely, you'll see that the hoop with the paper clip doesn't roll at an even speed. It seems to speed up as the paper clip circles down toward the ramp. Then it slows down when the clip climbs back up away from the ramp. Eventually the hoop with the paper clip loses.

Why:

It isn't friction that slows down the hoop with the paper clip. It slows down because it is out of balance. This is why auto garages balance the wheels on cars and trucks.

What now:

Let's see if we can remedy the situation. Tape a paper clip exactly opposite the first one and repeat the race.

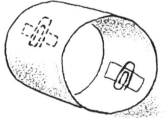

Add two more paper clips, each one halfway between the clips already in place. The hoop should roll better now.

Why:

Objects that turn, such as tires and engines, have to be as perfectly balanced as possible. Otherwise, they need more energy to turn and they don't turn easily. This causes extra wear and can even destroy them.

The Astounding Balancing Coin

When was the last time you saw someone balance a coin on a spinning coat hanger? For that matter, did you ever hear of anyone who tried such a stunt?

You need:

a washer or coin   a plastic coat hanger

What to do:

If you can't find one of those thick plastic coat hangers you can try this with a regular wire hanger—but you'll need a great sense of balance.

Now that you have your coat hanger, go outside. Since you're going to be experimenting outdoors, you're better off using a washer instead of a coin. A dropped coin that is easy to find on the living room floor may be lost outside.

Loop the hanger over your finger. With your other hand balance the washer or coin on the bottom of the hanger so it looks like this:

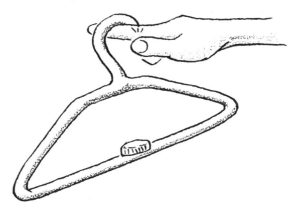

Now you know why it is a good idea to use the thick plastic hanger. It's not hard to balance a washer on a thick hanger, but it's a real chore to get it to balance on a thin wire one.

Be absolutely sure to place the coin directly below your finger, which is sticking through the hanger's hook.

Once the coin is balanced, begin rocking the hanger gently back and forth on your finger. Speed it up gradually.

When the hanger is swinging well, give it an extra spurt of energy and start it spinning in a circle around your finger.

What happens:

The coin will stay in place as long as you keep the hanger spinning and don't jerk it.

Don't be tempted to demonstrate this experiment in a room full of breakable things. If you happen to let the hanger slip off your finger, you better be outdoors!

Why:

Centrifugal force is created when things spin rapidly. It causes spinning things to try to move away from the center around which they are spinning. The coin is pressed against the bottom of the hanger by centrifugal force. It won't slip off unless you slow way down or break the smooth spinning motion.

The Spinning Bowl

Scientists demonstrate centrifugal force in huge laboratories. You can do it in your kitchen sink.

You need:

a large mixing bowl
or pot
a dessert bowl

a dish mop (if you
have one)

What to do:

Fill the large mixing bowl with about three or four inches (10 cm) of water. If you have a bowl that's about ten or twelve inches across (30 cm), it will be perfect for this experiment.

Float a dessert bowl inside the big bowl or pot.

Pour enough water into the floating dessert bowl to fill it one-fourth to three-eighths of an inch (1 cm) deep.

Now spin the floating bowl as rapidly as possible. If you have a dish mop at the sink, use that to spin the bowl. Just stick it into the bowl as shown here and begin turning it. If you don't have a dish mop, stick your index finger into the bowl to start it spinning. Since the bowl is floating, there is very little friction to slow it down and it will spin easily.

Use a little wrist motion and the dessert bowl will pick up speed.

Try to keep it centered in the larger bowl. If the bowls touch, the spinning one will slow down.

What happens:

Watch the water inside the floating bowl as you spin it faster and faster. The water will rise along its sides until the bottom of the spinning bowl is completely dry.

Let it slow down and the water will flow down from the sides of the bowl and cover the bottom again.

Why:

Centrifugal force works on liquids just as it does on solid things. The faster you spin an object, the more it wants to escape by flying to the outer edge of the circle.

Power-Lifting Fingers

Your fingers are a lot stronger than you think. This experiment demonstrates that power and is a great party stunt.

You need:

a straight chair   6 people

What to do:

One person sits erect in a straight-backed chair with hands clasped, head bent slightly forward and neck stiff. In fact, the sitting person's entire body should be as unbending as possible.

Have each of the other five people extend one index finger. It helps to steady this hand with the other hand like this:

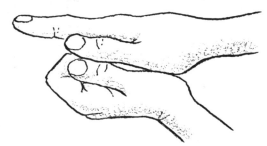

Ask one person to stand beside each of the sitting person's knees. Have them slip their entire index fingers under the sitter's knees.

Two other lifters will stand behind the chair and place their entire index fingers under the sitter's armpits.

The fifth lifter may stand beside the sitter or in front, placing an index finger under the sitter's chin.

Tell everyone to take a deep breath and hold it. Count, "One, two, three." All five lifters lift straight up on "Three." Caution everyone to lift straight up but not to jerk.

What happens:
To everyone's surprise the sitting person comes right up out of the chair. Be sure to caution the lifters not to let the person drop once he or she is in the air.

Why:
Since the sitter remains stiff, his or her weight is evenly distributed among all five lifters. By having everyone move at the same instant, the weight remains divided evenly, so everyone lifts the same amount.

So, if the sitter weighs eighty pounds (36 kg) this means each lifter only has to raise about sixteen (7 kg) of those pounds.

Pulley Power

If you want to pull a string instead of lifting a weight, a pulley is exactly what you need.

You need:

2 empty thread spools
2 chairs
10 feet (3 m) of strong
   string

a book
2 wire hangers
a broomstick
scissors

What to do:

To perform this experiment in motion and movement, you need to build some pulleys. An easy way to do this is to unwind the neck of a wire hanger. Push the end through the center of a thread spool (If you have to straighten the wire a bit to get it through the spool, that's fine.) Then bend it back into shape.

When you've fastened the hanger back together, your pulley looks like this:

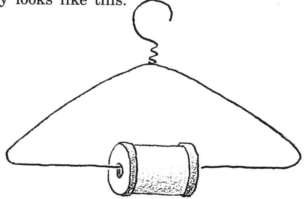

Make two pulleys while you're at it.

Hook one pulley to an overhead support. A good way to do this is to set two chairs back to back and place a broomstick between them. Then tie a loop of string around the stick to hold the pulley.

Cut a piece of string long enough to tie around the book, which is the load you are going to lift.

Cut another piece of string four feet (1.2 m) long. Tie it to the string on the book and run it over the pulley.

Now pull down on the string.

What happens:
The book rises.

Why:
Of course it did! What's so great about that? The great thing is that you changed the direction of motion. You pulled down and the book came up. This ability to change the direction of motion lets us set up factories and do the work needed to construct buildings and bridges.

In this experiment you pulled down just as hard as you would have to pull up to lift the book. You didn't gain any mechanical advantage using just one pulley. Turn the page and you'll find out how to get science to improve your lifting power.

Double Power

Here's your chance to be twice as strong as you were before.

You need:

The same items you used for the last project

What to do:

Leave the last experiment set up exactly as it was. Hook the second pulley into the string that is tied around the book you plan to lift. Things should be set up like this:

Now pull up on the string that runs around the second pulley. Measure the amount of string you pull up to lift the book three inches (7.5 cm).

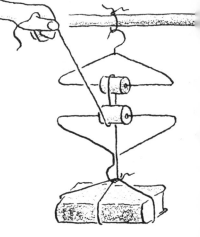

What happens:

You will be using less force to lift the book than you did using only one pulley. You'll also pull six inches (15 cm) of string through the pulleys to lift the book three inches (7.5 cm).

Why:

Using two pulleys gives you what we call a mechanical advantage. This simply means that it is easier to lift the book than it was before. However, you have to pull twice as much string through the pulleys to gain this advantage.

The Mysterious Moving Glass

Can you make a glass of water move without touching the glass?

You need:

2 glasses nearly full of water

a pencil
a ruler

What to do:

Fill both glasses nearly full of water. Place the pencil under the ruler as shown in the drawing. Set one glass of water at each end of the ruler. Hold onto each glass until it is balanced.

Now move the pencil along under the ruler until the raised end is almost ready to tip downward.

Place two fingers in the water but don't touch the glass. Push your fingers down into the water.

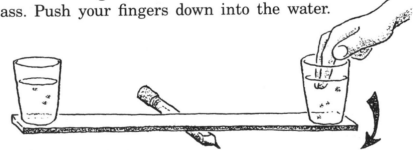

What happens:

As your fingers move down in the water, that glass will move down as shown by the arrow in the drawing. The level of the water will rise in the glass as your fingers push into the water.

Why:

As your fingers push into the water they move or displace water, which causes the water level to rise. The glass's weight is increased by exactly the amount of water that is displaced.

THE SOUND OF SCIENCE

Sounds are all around us. We are used to hearing the sound of other voices, a dog's bark, the honking of an automobile horn, or the slamming of a door.

In fact, sounds are so much a part of our daily lives that a sudden, total silence can be frightening. Total silence is so different from what we are used to that some people claim the silence itself creates sound.

Everyone knows how to create sound. Strike one hand against the other and you'll cause a sound to be made.

What actually causes the sound of two hands clapping? When two objects come together hard and fast to create a sound, they cause the air to move or vibrate—a result of the force of their coming together. This vibration of the air causes little waves of sound to travel out in all directions.

Some of those sound waves or vibrations reach your ear. They cause your eardrum to vibrate or move back and forth slightly. This movement causes the tiny bones inside your ear to pick up that vibration and relay it through a tiny tube of liquid to the hearing or auditory nerves. These nerves communicate the sound to your brain and you hear.

When we speak, our vocal cords vibrate in our throats. The force of the air coming out of our lungs and passing the vocal cords creates these vibrations. The moving vocal cords set air in motion and the sound is carried from our mouths.

If you'd like to test how this works, try to speak out loud while you are pulling air into your lungs. You can make a sound, but you can't speak when you breathe in. Try it now just to make sure.

Now let's check out some experiments in sound that are fun and that offer some surprises. They also help us understand how we hear.

Noisy Paper

Two sheets of notebook or typing paper make a great noisemaker.

You need:
2 sheets of notebook or typing paper
2 pieces of cellophane 2″ × 2″ (5 cm × 5 cm)

What to do:
Hold the two sheets of paper up in front of you. Make sure the bottom sheet sticks out toward you about a half inch (12.5 mm) past the top paper. They should look like this:

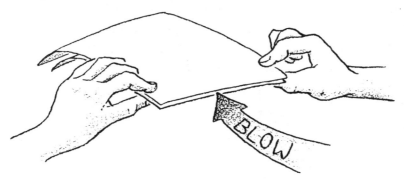

Now blow directly toward the two sheets at the point shown by the arrow.

What happens:
The two papers will make a strange, noisy sound.

If you don't get some sort of sound from the papers move your mouth closer and blow again. When you blow *between* the two sheets of paper they vibrate rapidly back and forth.

If you still haven't created a great sound, adjust the way you hold the papers. Move your fingers closer to your mouth or farther back. Blow harder or less hard. Eventually you'll find the right combination.

Don't blow until you get dizzy. Blow, then rest a few seconds.

Why:
When the papers flutter back and forth their vibration creates the sound you hear. Their vibration creates sound waves that your ear picks up.

The Screamer

Here's your chance to make all the noise you want and do it in the name of science.

You need:
A piece of cellophane 2 inches square
  (5 cm square)

What to do:
Hold the piece of cellophane stretched tightly between the thumbs and index fingers of both hands.

Place your hands directly in front of your face so the cellophane is right in front of your lips. The set-up looks like this:

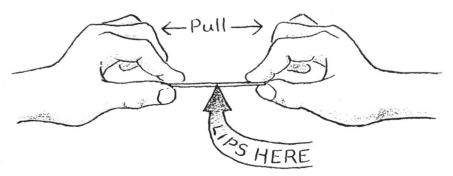

Blow hard and fast right at the edge of the tightly stretched piece of cellophane. Keep your lips close together so you send a thin stream of air right at the cellophane's edge.

What happens:

When the jet of air hits the edge of the cellophane you will create the greatest, most terrible sound you've ever heard!

If you don't get a terrible sound, adjust the distance between the cellophane and your lips until the air hits it just right.

Why:

The rapidly moving air from your lips causes the edge of the cellophane to vibrate quickly. Because the cellophane is extremely thin, the jet of air makes these vibrations *extremely* fast. The faster something vibrates the higher the tone it creates.

The Tapping Finger

Do you know how to make even the lightest taps of your finger sound loud?

You need:
a wooden table or desk top

What to do:
Sit at the table or desk. Place your ear flat on top like this:

Tap with your finger on the surface of the table about a foot away from your ear. Tap hard. Then tap softly.

What happens:
The sound of your tapping finger is much louder than when you listen to the same tapping with your head not touching the table. Check right now to be sure this is true.

Why:
Sound waves don't *only* travel through air. They also travel through solids, such as a table or desk. Many solids—such as wood—carry sound waves much better than air. This is why your tapping finger sounds louder when you hear it through wood than through air.

Balloon Amplifier

You're used to seeing big sound amplifiers that make sounds louder. We often call these amplifiers "speakers." But did you know a balloon can increase the volume of sound?

You need:
a balloon

What to do:
Blow up an ordinary party balloon. The round type is perfect. A longer sausage balloon will do, though, if that's the only kind you have handy.

Hold the blown-up balloon right against your ear like this:

Tap lightly on the side of the balloon away from your face.

Do not do anything that will make the balloon pop while it's next to your ear. The loud noise of an exploding balloon won't do your ear any good at all.

What happens:
The sound you hear is lots louder than the light tapping of your finger.

Why:
The air inside the balloon is tightly compressed. This means the air molecules are much closer to each other inside the balloon than they are in the air in the rest of the room. When you blew up the balloon you actually let your lungs work as an air compressor, forcing the air to expand the rubber balloon.

We've already discovered that wood conducts sound well. This is because the molecules in wood are closer together than the molecules in air.

When you crowded the molecules closer together inside the balloon, that air became a better conductor of sound waves than ordinary air.

The Spoon That Thinks It's a Bell

How can a spoon act like a bell? Read on and find out.

You need:

a teaspoon
4 feet (1.2 m) of string
scissors

a soup spoon
a table or chair
a serving spoon

What to do:

Cut a piece of ordinary string about four feet (1.2 m) long. Tie a simple sliding loop in the middle of the string. Do this by simply wrapping one end of the string over the other and pulling the open loop down so that it is halfway between the ends of the string.

Don't tighten the loop into a knot. Leave it open about half an inch like this:

Slip the handle of a teaspoon through the loop and tighten the loop so the spoon won't slip out. Adjust the spoon so it hangs with the scoop end just a little lower than the handle.

Now press one end of the string against the outside of your right ear and the other string end against the outside of your left ear. Don't put the string into your ear.

Next, swing the string gently so that the scoop of the spoon hits the edge of a table or the back of a chair. Listen to the sound you hear.

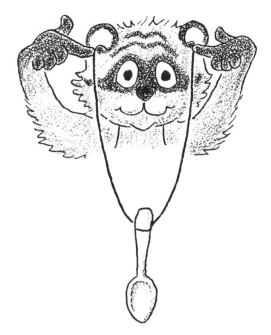

What happens:

By swinging the spoon gently you will hear a sound that is nothing like a spoon striking a table. It's more like a bell. In fact, it's like a church bell.

Why:

The string conducts the vibration of the spoon. Not only does string carry sound waves better than air, it directs them right into your ear. This accounts for the deep bell-like tone you hear.

What now:

Repeat this experiment using a soup spoon and listen to the deeper tone it creates.

Then, give your ears a treat, and do it with a serving spoon. Because of its greater size its sound is much deeper.

The Listening Yardstick

Did you ever try to hear through a yardstick? Now's the time!

You need:
a yardstick   a ticking clock

What to do:
A wind-up alarm clock is perfect for this experiment. If you don't have one, then check your electric alarm clock. Does it make a whirring sound? Most of them do if you listen carefully. If it doesn't, find some other appliance in the house that hums or makes a mechanical sound that isn't very loud.

Hold the yardstick so that one end touches the clock and the other end presses against your ear.

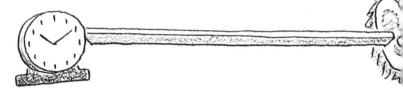

If you don't have a yardstick, a ruler will work. So will a wooden dowel rod.

Don't poke yourself in the ear. Press the end of the yardstick against the outside of your ear.

What happens:
The sound of the clock is much louder now than when you listen to it without the yardstick. You can check this by using the yardstick to listen to other appliances around the house.

Why:
The wooden yardstick carries sound waves better

than air. Therefore, you hear the clock's sounds more loudly through the yardstick than when you listen normally.

The Strange Vibrating Bowl

Can you hear the sounds from a vibrating bowl? Let's find out.

You need:

a bottle
a table
a bowl
a dinner fork

a pencil with an
  eraser
3 feet of string (1 m)

What to do:

Set the bottle on the table. A two-liter soft drink bottle is great, but you may need to remove the cap since it is not perfectly flat. A salad oil bottle works just as well.

Don't choose your family's best china soup bowl for this experiment. Use one that isn't supposed to break with normal use.

Balance the bowl upside down on top of the bottle like this:

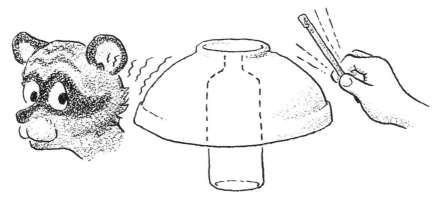

Put your ear close to the bowl and tap the edge of the bowl with the eraser end of the pencil. Better still, have a friend do the tapping.

Then repeat the experiment but this time have your friend touch the edge of the bowl with his or her finger.

What happens:
The first time you'll hear a pleasant sound. The second time, when your friend touches the edge of the bowl, you won't hear it.

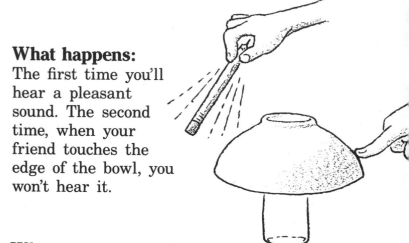

Why:
The sound is created because the bowl is vibrating. When your friend touches the bowl with a finger tip that causes the vibration to stop and the sound to end.

Can You Tune a Fork?

It's sad but true that you can tune a piano but no one can tune a fork. However, even an untuned fork is good for a tone, if not a tune.

You need:
a dinner fork
a pencil with an
    eraser

3 feet of string (1 m)
a soup bowl

What now:

Tie one end of the string around a dinner fork as shown in the drawing. Lift the fork by the string so that the tines hang straight down.

Tap the bowl with the pencil and lower the fork so that its tines are lightly touching the opposite side of the bowl.

What happens:

When the fork touches the bowl its tines begin to vibrate. If you hold your ear close to the tines you can probably hear the tone.

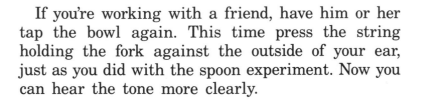

If you're working with a friend, have him or her tap the bowl again. This time press the string holding the fork against the outside of your ear, just as you did with the spoon experiment. Now you can hear the tone more clearly.

Why:

The fork tines pick up the vibrations from the bowl. This is called "sympathetic" vibration. The string helps conduct the sound, just as it did with the spoon that thought it was a bell.

Tuning a Glass

We found you can't tune a fork, but who said anything about tuning a glass?

You need:

8 drinking glasses   a pencil
  or glass bottles   water

What to do:

Line up the eight drinking glasses or glass bottles in a row on the kitchen counter. (Plastic bottles won't work this time.)

It does not matter if the glasses are all the same size or not. If they are, though, it's quicker to tune them.

Fill the glasses part full of water, so that they look pretty much like those in the drawing.

As you see, each glass has a little less water in it than the one to its left.

Now use the pencil to gently but firmly strike the side of each glass.

What happens:

You will hear a different tone from each of the glasses. The more water there is in a glass, the lower the tone that it makes.

Call the first glass on your left "do," which is the first note of the musical scale. Strike the next glass. If its tone is the next step up the scale move on. If not, either add a bit of water or pour some out until that glass's tone is one step up from the first.

Keep on in this manner until you have tuned the eight glasses to play a musical scale.

Why:

We know that vibrations cause sound. Striking the side of a glass causes it to vibrate. The speed of the vibration depends upon how much glass and water there are to set in motion. The more water, the slower the vibrations and the deeper the tone.

What now:

Set up eight glasses that are different in size. The more different, the better.

Keep in mind that it is the total amount of water that determines the tone of the glass.

Now tune these eight glasses to play a musical scale by adding or pouring out water until each tone is one step above the one to its left.

Seeing Sound Waves

Now's your chance to see sound waves.

You need:

an empty can   scissors
a small mirror   glue
newspaper   a hammer
a balloon

What to do:

Cut both ends from a tin food can. Wash the can carefully with warm water and soap. Watch out for sharp edges left from the can opener.

Next you need a piece of balloon to fit over one end of the can. It's a good idea to blow up the balloon and play with it a while before stretching it over the can. This makes the rubber easier to pull. Then let the air out and cut the neck off the balloon with the scissors. Stretch a piece of the main part of the balloon over one end of the can. Hold it in place with a rubber band. You'll probably have to wrap the rubber band around the balloon and can several times.

You need a small piece of reflecting material. A bit of mirror would be perfect but don't break a good mirror. If you don't have an old mirror, use a piece of aluminum foil. It's easy to cut and glue, though it usually gives a fuzzy reflection. If you're using an old mirror, wrap it in several sheets of newspaper. Then, tap it with a hammer. Unwrap the newspaper and carefully pick out a piece of mirror about half an inch (12.5 mm) square. Wrap up the other scraps in the paper and throw them away.

Use a drop of glue to fasten the mirror to the balloon as shown here.

Stand so the sunlight from a window hits the reflector. Move the can around until the reflection shows up on a wall, like this:

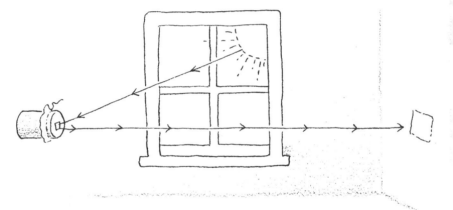

Talk directly into the open end of the can. Shout. Make different sounds. Watch the reflection.

What happens:
The sounds you make cause movement.

Why:
The rubber on the can picks up the vibrations of the sound waves from your voice. As it vibrates, so does the reflector. That's what makes the reflection on the wall move.

FEELING STRESSED? TRY SOME SURFACE TENSION

Water is an extremely important part of our lives. Without it, human life cannot survive.

Not only do we drink water, but the major part of our bodies is also composed of water.

We bathe in it, we sail across it, we use it as the basis for drinks ranging from sodas and juices to tea and coffee.

Without water we'd have no trees, no grass, no flowers—no life as we know it. In short, water is essential to living.

In this chapter we'll find out some interesting facts about water. We'll see that it can do some amazing things, and that it's great to experiment with. We'll find out something else about water. You've probably heard a lot about tension and stress. Water also has tension, but of a different type than the one that comes with stress.

Water has surface tension. Surface tension is a scientific term that means that the surface of a bowl of water has the ability to hold itself together. This happens because the molecules that make up a container of water tend to cling to one another.

Normally, we don't think of a lake or ocean as having water molecules clinging together to form a covering for the water. But that is exactly what surface tension does. You don't feel it when you poke your finger into a cup of water or when you dive into a swimming pool. But it exists, even if you are not aware of it.

Let's begin this chapter with some experiments that show some of the surprising things water does because of surface tension. Then we'll move on to some really interesting things below the surface.

Full to Overflowing

Everyone has filled a glass or cup until it flows over the top. Here's your chance to fill a glass to overflowing without spilling a drop.

You need:

a glass of water   lots of pins

What to do:

Set a glass of water on the table. Add water until it is full to the brim.

Now to answer this question: How many pins can you drop into the glass before it runs over? Ten? Twenty? Fifty?

Carefully hold a pin over the glass so that its point just touches the surface of the water.

Let go of the pin so it slides into the water. Add another pin and then another until the water finally runs over.

What happens:

You'll add more pins than you believed possible. Look sideways at the glass and you'll see the level of the water is above the edge of the glass.

Why:

Surface tension keeps the water from overflowing long after it seems possible for the glass to hold any more pins.

The Strange Expanding Loop of Thread

Once we do something to change water's surface tension, strange things happen.

You need:
a bowl of water

a bar of soap

a foot or so of thread (.3 m)

What to do:
Fill the bowl of water nearly to the top.

Form the thread into a loop by lapping one end over the other. Don't make a knot in the thread. Carefully place the loop on the surface of the water. Keep the loop sort of skinny so it looks like this:

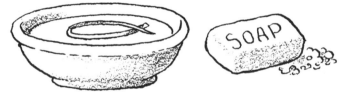

Now touch the corner of a bar of soap to the water inside the loop in the thread.

What happens:
The loop will form a circle around the soap.

Why:
The soap destroys the surface tension of the water inside the loop. The thread keeps the soap from spreading beyond the loop. Since the water outside the loop still has its surface tension, it pulls away, taking the thread with it. This leaves you with a circular loop around the soap.

The Stubborn Cork

Can a cork be stubborn? Here's how to deal with one that refuses to obey your commands.

You need:

a cork or a small
   piece of wood
a glass of water
a spoon

What to do:

Fill the glass of water nearly to the top. Now float a cork or a piece of wood in the glass. Within a short time the cork will drift to the side of the glass.

Your challenge is to convince the cork to come to the center of the glass without touching it or taking it out of the water. If you want to blow on it, that's okay, but once it reaches the center of the glass it must stay there after you stop blowing.

Here's how to make the stubborn cork obey. Slowly, a spoonful at a time, begin to add water to the glass. Eventually the water will rise above the top of the glass as surface tension holds it in place.

What happens:

The cork drifts to the center of the glass and stays there when the water level rises high enough.

Why:

Surface tension lets the water rise above the glass. It causes the water to form a little curved dome whose high point is at its center. The cork seeks the highest point of the water.

A Strainer Full of Water

A strainer won't hold water. Or will it?

You need:

cooking oil   a small strainer
an empty bowl   a glass of water

What to do:

Begin with a small strainer because large ones call for too much cooking oil. A tea strainer is best.

Coat the strainer with cooking oil. A good way to do this is to pour the oil into the bowl and then gently slosh the strainer around in the bowl until it is coated with oil.

Shake the strainer carefully into the bowl so that all the holes are open.

Don't throw away the cooking oil you just used. If you set it aside, you can use it in the experiment on page 88.

Hold the strainer over the sink. Start pouring water very, very slowly from the glass into the strainer.

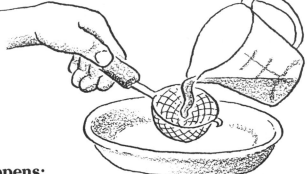

What happens:

As you carefully pour the water, you'll see the strainer begin to fill with water. Look closely and you'll see tiny beads of water pushing through the wires, but very few of them will leak out.

Why:
Again it is the surface tension of the beads of water that makes this experiment work. The oil helps by giving the wires a smooth coating. It also makes the spaces between the wires a fraction smaller, because, even after you shake the oil off, some of it clings to the wires.

The Incredible Upside Down Bottle

Anyone can turn a bottle of water upside down. But how many people can do it without having the water spill out?

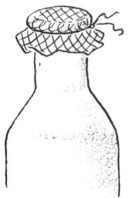

You need:
a bottle
   with a small mouth and neck
a small piece of screening
   or a strainer
6 inches (15 cm) of soft wire
   or a rubber band
a friend to help

What to do:
This experiment really needs at least three hands some of the time. Unless you happen to have an extra hand yourself, make sure you have a friend around who can help when needed.

Fill the bottle (a soft drink bottle is ideal, but any bottle shaped the same way will work) with water all the way to the top.

Cover the mouth of the bottle with screen wire, if you have a little chunk of screening available. If not, check to see if you have any plastic screen of the type that comes in some frozen dinner cooking pouches.

Attach the screen to the top of the bottle with a piece of wire or a rubber band.

If you don't have a piece of screen available, you can hold a strainer tightly against the mouth of the bottle. That's where you need that extra hand your friend will supply.

With the screen in place or the strainer held tightly against the bottle's mouth, quickly turn the bottle upside down.

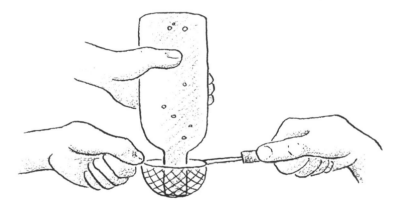

What happens:

The water doesn't run out. Just be sure, if you're using a strainer, to hold it absolutely tight against the mouth of the bottle. Otherwise, you'll spring a leak.

Why:

Surface tension is helping. It also helps that the bottle is full so that no air is trapped inside the bottle to push down on the water. The only direction air pressure is pushing is up against the water that might want to run through the screen.

The Hawk and the Sparrows

Hawks often fly into a flock of sparrows and scatter them. You'll see why this experiment was named for them when you complete it.

You need:
a dinner plate filled
  with water

a bar of soap
talcum powder

What to do:
Fill a dinner plate nearly full of water. Place the plate on the table and pour water into it.

When the water is calm, sprinkle a bit of the powder onto the surface of the water—just a pinch of it between your thumb and finger.

The powder will float on the water like this:

The bits of powder are the "sparrows."

Rub the tip of your finger on a bar of soap. Touch the surface of the water with your finger tip. Your finger is the "hawk."

What happens:
The instant your soapy finger touches the water the powder "sparrows" scatter.

Why:
The soap breaks the surface tension of the water. The water around the edges of the dish pulls away and carries the powder with it.

A Scale You Never Thought Of

Can you use a bowl of water as a scale?

You need:

a baking pan

an apple, an orange or
   other piece of fruit

a large bowl of water

a measuring cup

What to do:

Set the bowl in the baking pan. Fill the bowl to the rim with water. Select an apple, an orange or any piece of fruit you want to weigh. Place it in the bowl of water.

What happens:

Water will overflow into the baking pan.

Carefully lift the bowl of water out of the pan. Pour the water from the pan into the measuring cup. Read the scale on the side of the cup to see how many ounces of water are in it. This reading gives you the weight of the fruit.

Why:

The water that overflowed was displaced by the fruit. The amount of water a floating object displaces is the same as the object's weight.

Water's Great Escape

You've heard that water doesn't run uphill. Here's an experiment that shows how you can coax water into it.

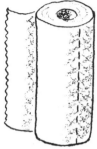

You need:
a glass nearly full of water

a bowl

2 paper towels

What to do:
Just in case there's a leak, it's a good idea to do this experiment in the kitchen sink.

Fill a glass nearly full of water. Set it beside an empty bowl. You can place both the glass and the bowl on a pizza pan instead of in the sink, if you'd rather.

The plan is to have the water move up and over the rim of the glass and down into the bowl. In order to do this we need a wick through which the water can travel.

A wick is a tight roll of paper or cloth that will absorb water. Just as a candle wick carries melted wax up to the flame, our water wick will carry water along its length.

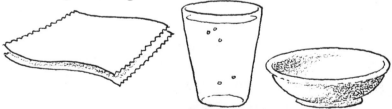

Pull off two paper towels and twist them together fairly tightly to form the wick. Bend the wick in the middle. Then place one end in the glass. Be sure the other end reaches into the bowl, like this:

If you don't have paper towels handy, a clean cloth handkerchief makes a good wick. Just twist it into a tight roll.

What happens:

Within just a minute or so you'll see the wick getting wet as water begins to travel along it. After a few minutes some water will appear in the bottom of the bowl.

Water won't flow from the glass into the bowl. Instead of flowing, it sort of oozes. This experiment takes time. Check back once in a while to see how it is coming.

When the water level in the bowl is as high as that left in the glass, the water stops moving. If you set the glass on something higher than the bowl you can get most of the water out of it.

Why:

There are thousands and maybe even millions of tiny spaces between the fibers of the paper towel or the handkerchief. Water moves into these openings and advances along the twisted material. Its movement is known as capillary action. Moisture moves from plant roots into the rest of the plant in this same way.

Slow But Mighty

Is it possible for a can full of cardboard squares to lift a heavy board?

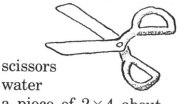

You need:

an empty tin can
dishwasher detergent
2 or 3 empty cereal
  boxes

scissors
water
a piece of 2×4 about
  two feet (.6 m) long

What to do:

Wash out the empty can with soap and water. Watch out for sharp metal around the edge.

Cut enough square pieces of cereal box cardboard to fill the can when you stack the pieces on top of each other. Don't worry about making the pieces of cardboard the exact size of the can. It's better and faster to cut them a bit smaller, like this:

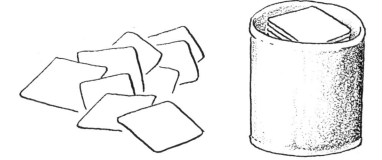

When the stack of cardboard pieces fills the can, most of your work is done.

Now fill the can with water. It will speed things up if you add a squirt of dishwasher detergent or a bit of dishwasher powder. Don't use dish soap—you can do without bubbles.

Within a minute or so you'll see that the water level has dropped as much as an inch. This is because the water is seeping into the pieces of cardboard. Add enough water to bring the water level back to the top of the can.

Push down on the cardboard. You can probably add a few more pieces.

Now place the 2×4 on top of the can like this:

You can use any fairly heavy weight that is unbreakable if you don't have a 2×4 handy.

What happens:
Within a short time the piece of wood or other heavy item will begin to rise. When it stops rising, remove it and try to push the cardboard back into the can. This will be difficult, if not impossible!

Why:
Capillary action causes the water to soak into the pieces of cardboard. Once each piece of cardboard fills with water it is a fraction thicker than it was without the water. This is what causes the lifting action which raised the piece of 2×4.

The Case of the Shrinking Tissues

Facial tissues don't get smaller and smaller—or do they? Here's an experiment that asks the question: What happened to the tissues?

You need:

part of a box of facial tissues

pencil or dinner knife

a glass of water

What to do:

Fill a glass with water until the water comes to about a quarter of an inch or a bit more (9 mm) below the top of the glass.

Pull six facial tissues from their box. Tear each one into strips one inch to one and a half inches (3.75 cm) wide. The dotted lines in the illustration show where to tear the tissues.

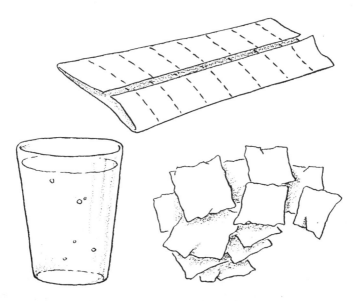

Don't worry if you don't tear them straight.

Now, one strip of tissue at a time, stuff it into the glass of water. Use a pencil or the tip of a dinner knife to keep pressing the tissues down toward the bottom of the glass.

What happens:

You'll probably see small bubbles rise through the water from time to time. This is because some air was trapped by the tissue when you pushed it into the water.

As you push the tissues down with the pencil or knife you free the trapped air. This makes room for more tissues in the water.

Why:

Highly absorbent items such as facial tissues have only a little bit of solid material in them. They are made up largely of air space.

Once the air is gone from the tissues there isn't a lot left. This is why you can stuff so many into the glass of water. Cotton balls work the same way.

The Moving Mystery Match

Why does a wooden match suddenly decide to move?

You need:

a wooden match   a coin
water   a spoon

What to do:

Bend a wooden match in half. Don't break it in two pieces. Leave several wood fibers holding it together. Place the coin so that just its edges rest on the match.

Run a few drops of water into the spoon. Let a single drop of water fall onto the broken match at the point shown by the arrow.

What happens:

Almost instantly the two halves of the match will move apart slightly and the coin will fall off at least one of the halves.

Why:

Water causes wood fibers to expand or swell, which makes the match move slightly.

What now:

If you want to use this experiment to impress your friends, set it up so that the match rests on the rim of a bottle. Just be sure the neck of the bottle is large enough so that the coin falls into the bottle when the match moves.

You Can't Keep a Good Button Down

If you've ever wanted to see a button rise and fall in a glass of liquid, now's your chance.

You need:

a shirt button—or one no larger than ¾ of an inch across (18 mm) across

a glass
soda

What to do:

Fill a glass with any carbonated soda. One of the clear sodas is probably best because you can see through it easily. Leave about half an inch (12.5 mm) of space at the top of the glass.

Drop the button into the glass. If it wants to float on top of the soda, give it a tap with your finger and send it to the bottom of the glass.

What happens:

Small bubbles begin to form around the button.

Suddenly the button rises to the top of the glass. Give it a tap to knock the little gas bubbles off and it will sink to the bottom again.

This will go on so long as the soda is fizzy. If you wish you can have several buttons rising and falling in the same glass.

Why:

The gas bubbles are carbon dioxide, which is what gives soda its "fizz." When they attach to the button they give it enough lift or buoyancy to make it rise.

The Great Cooking Oil Trade Off

Can you trade a glass of cooking oil for one of water without pouring one into the other?

You need:

two small glasses the
  same size
scissors
cookie sheet

cooking oil
cereal box cardboard
a friend

What to do:

Begin with two glasses exactly the same size. Juice glasses are perfect.

Cut a piece of cereal box cardboard about three or four inches (7.5–10 cm) square, large enough so that when you place it over the mouth of a glass, it sticks out ¾ of an inch (18 mm) on each side.

Fill one of the glasses to the brim with water. Fill the other to the brim with cooking oil. For safety's sake, set both on a cookie sheet.

Place the cardboard on top of the glass of water. Hold it firmly in place and turn the glass over so it looks like this:

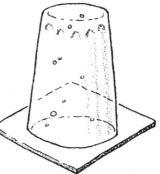

Set the upside down glass of water with the cardboard still in place on top of the glass of cooking oil. Don't let the cardboard slip!

Hold both glasses steady and slowly move the cardboard sideways. Here's where your friend comes in. You need an extra hand to hold things in place. Move the cardboard until its edge is exactly where the rims of the glasses meet, like this:

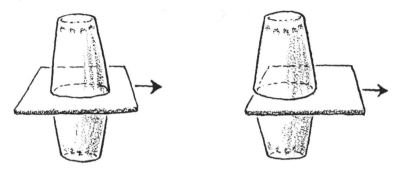

If a drop of water leaks out, don't worry about it. Pull the cardboard very slowly another eighth of an inch or so. There is now an opening between the water on top and the oil below.

What happens:

A few oil bubbles rise into the water glass. They will form a little oil dome on the bottom of the water glass (which is at the top, of course).

Pull the cardboard a bit farther and suddenly you'll see the oil begin to roll upward into the water glass. At the same time, water flows down to replace the oil.

In a minute or less the top glass is full of oil and the water is in the bottom glass.

Why:

Because water is heavier than cooking oil, the water flows downward, forcing the lighter weight oil upward. This is why oil and water don't mix and oil floats on water.

SCIENCE CAN GIVE YOU A WARM FEELING

Light is something we take for granted. The sun shines. We turn on an electric light. Light shines through glass. It is light that enables us to see reflections in mirrors.

Light travels in rays that move in a straight line at great speed. When we speak of the speed of light we are talking about a light ray that travels through space at 186,000 miles (297,600 km) per second! To get a good idea of what this speed means, consider that the Sun is 93,000,000 miles (148,800,000 km) away from us. Light travels from the Sun to the earth in just about eight minutes.

Even though light rays travel in straight lines, these rays can be bent or refracted. When light enters water or passes through glass the light ray bends at an angle. Once it leaves the glass or water the ray again moves in a straight line. However, it is traveling at a different angle than before it encountered the glass or the water.

Our chief source of light is from the Sun. However, we create light by artificial means, such as electricity, as well.

An important thing to remember about light is that it is related to heat. It's the Sun's tremendous heat that causes it to give off light. A burning fire also creates light. If you hold your hand near, but not touching, an electric light bulb you'll feel the heat it gives off.

Heat can also cause light. It is the heating of the filament or insides of an electric light that creates the artificial light we see from a bulb.

When things are heated enough, they change. Vegetables become tender from cooking. A room gets warm when the furnace comes on. Ice melts and water boils if heated enough. Air and many other materials expand when heated. It is the expansion of air that makes some of the experiments in this chapter work.

Breaking Up Rays of Sunlight

It's possible to break up or separate the Sun's rays. When this is done, a ray of light suddenly shows a rainbow of colors. And you can do it in about two minutes.

You need:

a baking pan or soup
  bowl
a small mirror

water
a sheet of white paper

What to do:

Run about an inch of water into the baking pan or soup bowl. This is going to take the place of the solid glass prism you have probably seen at school.

Now you need a small mirror. A hand mirror such as the one that fits in a small purse is perfect. This mirror will help the water break up light rays into bands of color, just as a prism does.

Set the water where sunlight shines directly on it, either indoors or outside.

Lean the mirror against one edge of the pan or bowl, like this:

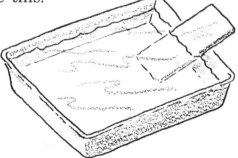

Direct the mirror's reflection onto a white ceiling or wall or a sheet of white paper. If you are outside, you'll probably need to use the paper as your viewing screen.

What happens:

You'll see a rainbow of colors on the ceiling or wall or sheet of paper. These colors start with red and end with violet.

Why:

Water causes the rays of sunlight reflected from the mirror to bend. When light rays bend, each color in the ray bends at a different angle. This causes the rainbow effect.

All the colors we normally see—such as red, orange, yellow, green, blue, and violet—are contained in sunlight. We see objects as having color depending upon which light rays they reflect. In the case of a prism, we get to see a rainbow because all the colors are reflected.

Upside Down In a Spoon

How can a spoon turn you upside down? This experiment is great fun for younger children you need to entertain.

You need:
a shiny soup or serving spoon

What to do:
The scoop of a spoon makes an interesting mirror. Just make sure the spoon you use is shiny and the larger the better. Hold the spoon up so that you see yourself in the scoop.

What happens:
When you look at the spoon you'll see your reflection upside down. Tip the spoon so it reflects other things that also appear upside down.

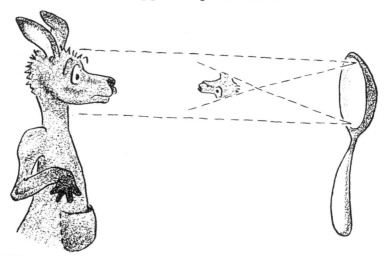

Why:
Light rays travel in straight lines. They are reflected in straight lines as well. But when light is

reflected from a curved surface, the rays leave the surface at different angles. The illustration below shows how this works with the spoon. The reflected image appears upside down because of the angle of the reflected rays of light.

The Case of the Vanishing Reflection

In this experiment you'll see your reflection one minute and have it vanish the next.

You need:
8 or 10 inches (20–25 cm) of smooth kitchen foil
scissors

What to do:
Use the scissors to cut a piece of kitchen foil off the roll. Don't tear it. Cut it. This avoids wrinkles.

Look at your reflection on the shiny side of the foil. It won't be perfect but you'll see yourself clearly.

Now crinkle the foil into a loose wad. Don't press it together tightly because you'll have to straighten it out again.

Flatten out the wadded foil, like this:

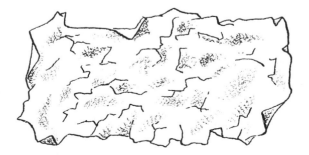

Now look for your reflection.

What happens:
No matter how you turn the foil you won't see your reflection. It has vanished.

Why:
Remember that light rays are reflected from a surface in straight lines. The once-smooth foil surface is now a mass of ridges and valleys. The reflected light bounces off in all directions.

Because these reflected rays are going off at different angles, your image does not form the way it did when its smooth surface reflected the rays right back at you.

A Water Droplet Magnifier

Yes, it's possible to make a tiny drop of water into a magnifier. You can't use it to read with, but it will magnify one letter at a time.

You need:
a thin wire or paper clip
a glass of water

a nail
pliers
a newspaper page

What to do:
Form a small loop in the end of a piece of thin wire. Make this loop as round as possible. A good way to do this is to bend the end of the wire around a nail.

If you use wire as stiff as a paper clip, you'll need a pair of pliers to form the loop. Paper clips are hard to bend when you work with just the end of a clip.

The loop should be about one-eighth of an inch (3 mm) across or just a tiny bit larger.

Dip the loop into a glass of water. You'll see that a film of water fills the inside of the loop. Tap the wire against the side of the glass. This helps form the tiny lens of water.

Hold the loop above a letter on the newspaper page.

What happens:

If all went well, the letter you're looking at will appear several times larger than it is.

If the letter seems smaller than usual, the water formed the wrong kind of lens. Tap it against the side of the glass and look again.

If you lose the water inside the loop, just dip the wire again and collect a new water lens.

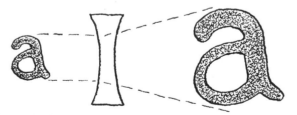

Why:

The drawing above shows how light enters and leaves the lens you just made. Always remember that light rays may be bent by a lens, but they always enter or leave the lens in a straight line.

The Hot Water Tap Always Leaks

It wastes water to have any tap leak. But it's even worse to realize that it is always the hot water tap that seems to be leaking.

You need:
2 paper cups
a pin

2 juice glasses

What to do:
Two paper cups such as you get at a fast food restaurant are perfect for this project. Wash them out carefully to get rid of any soft drink that remains.

Right in the middle of the bottom of each cup make a tiny pin hole. Then set the paper cups on top of the glasses like this:

Fill one cup half full of cold water. Drop in a couple of ice cubes to make sure it is really cold.

Fill the other cup half full of hot water out of the hot water tap.

Now sit back and observe the tiny drips from the pin holes in the bottoms of the cups.

What happens:
If the holes are the same size, you'll see the hot wa-

ter leaking faster than the cold. In fact, if the cold water is cold enough it may not leak at all.

Why:
The molecules in hot water move much faster than they do in cold water. The faster they move, the easier it is for them to slip past each other. That's why hot water is more likely to leak than cold.

Undersea Water Fountain

What happens when warm water suddenly appears beneath a mass of cold water?

You need:
a pot or kettle of cold water
a small bottle, glass if possible
ink, food color,
    or paint from watercolors

What to do:
Fill a pot or small kettle nearly full of cold water. It doesn't need to be ice water, but the colder the better. If you want, instead of using a kettle, just put the stopper in the kitchen sink and run about five inches (12.5 cm) of cold water into it.

Next, fill a small bottle about three-fourths full of hot water. A glass bottle works best, but if you only have a plastic bottle, it will do. Drop a couple of clean nuts or washers or marbles into the bottle. These will give it enough weight so it won't float when you put it into the cold water.

Add a few drops of ink or food color to the hot water. If you don't have any, then use a bit of paint from a set of watercolors.

Immediately put the bottle in the sink or on the bottom of the pot or kettle.

What happens:

The colored water will rise upward from the bottle towards the surface of the cold water. It looks just like a little underwater volcano erupting. Once the colored water begins to cool, it will thin out and settle towards the bottom of the pot.

Why:

Hot water rises because the molecules in it are moving rapidly. As they bounce and dart about they expand the water. When water or air expands, it gets less dense, because the same amount of matter takes up a larger space.

This expansion causes warm water or air to rise above colder, denser water or air. This sort of movement is called convection, by the way.

What a Way to Cut an Ice Cube

If you ever need to cut an ice cube in half, here's a way of doing it that has a result so surprising it seems impossible.

You need:

2 round pieces of wood (dowel rods) or 2 bolts 6–8 inches long (15–20 cm)

an ice cube
1½ feet (.45 m) of thin wire

What to do:

Tie the ends of the wire to the round pieces of wood. Dowel rods are perfect but so are pieces of broomstick. Fairly long bolts will work well, also.

If you don't have wire handy, thin nylon cord, such as a fishing leader, works all right.

Make sure the wire is tied tightly to the wood rods or bolts. You'll use them as handholds so you don't cut your fingers instead of the ice cube. The cutter looks like this:

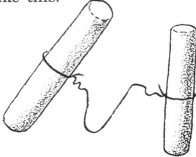

Next place the cube of ice on something solid that is high enough so you can stand over the cube and push down on the cutting tool. (I placed my ice cube on the porch deck rail, for instance.) Several short pieces of 2×4 lumber work well when stacked on top of each other. You can use a tin can as a cutting stand, too.

After placing the cube on the wood or can or whatever, position the cutting tool like this:

Take hold of the two handles and press down good and hard. Move the wire back and forth over the surface of the ice cube in a sawing motion while you keep pressing down.

What happens:

Within a few seconds the wire will begin to work its way slowly into the ice cube. As you continue to push down and the wire cuts deeper, you may wish to stop the back and forth motion and just keep pressing down.

The wire sinks into the ice cube even if you don't keep up the sawing motion! And the amazing thing is that the ice cube seems to freeze over above the wire.

When the wire is nearly through the ice cube, let up just a bit on the downward pressure. This keeps the wire from coming through the bottom of the cube with a sudden jolt.

When the wire is finally all the way through the cube wouldn't you think you'd have two cubes? You don't. You still have only one cube because the two halves froze together.

Why:
Pressure on the wire causes the ice under the wire to melt. This is because pressure creates heat. However, the ice cube is cold enough to refreeze once the water oozes its way to the top of the wire where there is no pressure.

What now:
Hang two heavy weights on either end of the wire. Then stand back and watch the wire work its way through the ice cube all by itself.

The Hot Air Twirler

Here's a twirling toy that uses the heat from your hands for power.

You need:
a piece of paper 3×3 inches
  (7.5 cm × 7.5 cm)
scissors

a pin
a pencil with an eraser

What to do:
Begin with a sheet of the thinnest paper you can find. Cut a square that is exactly three by three inches (7.5 cm × 7.5 cm).

Fold the square diagonally and then unfold it.

The solid line in the illustration shows this fold. The dotted line shows the next fold to make.

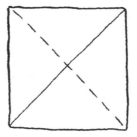

Once the two diagonal folds are in place, push in a little on opposite sides of the paper. This causes the center to rise about half an inch (1.25 cm) higher than the sides. The arrows in the illustration below show where to push.

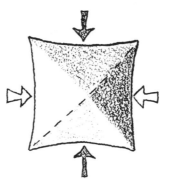

Next, push a straight pin into the eraser of a pencil. Leave an inch of the pin sticking straight up from the eraser. Then sit down and hold the pencil between your knees as seen in the drawing on page 105.

Set the square of paper on top of the pencil so that the head of the pin is right at the center peak, where the two folds come together.

Place your cupped hands on either side of the paper so they are about an inch or so away from it.

Now just sit and think warm thoughts without moving your hands or knees.

What happens:

Within just a minute the little paper twirler will begin to turn. If you see that the corner of the paper is going to hit your hands when it turns, move your hands back enough to give it room. Keep your hands as close to the paper as possible, however.

Once it gets going, the twirler will spin slowly around and around. The lighter the paper and the warmer your hands, the faster it turns.

Why:

The warmth from your hands heats the air near them. Heated air rises. The rising air causes the delicately balanced twirler to spin.

Blown Away

Air is all around us. We breathe it. We see things in the air such as dust, smoke, and the other kinds of pollution we all dread.

Air is moving constantly. We are aware of it when the wind blows. We also see clouds moving rapidly across the sky or watch a plume of smoke or steam as the wind blows it one way or the other.

When the speed of moving air increases, a number of things happen. Strong winds are very noticeable. But perhaps just as important is what happens when things move through the air.

Automotive engineers design cars so their movement through the air will be smooth. Airplanes fly only because air provides the "lift" necessary for them to remain in flight. It is the shape of their wings that changes the wind speed and results in the lifting effect.

Air also exerts pressure. Anyone who has ever tried to carry a large sheet of cardboard when the wind is blowing knows how great that pressure can be. And it is the force or pressure of moving air that drives a sailboat across the water.

Air doesn't need to move to exert pressure. Every minute it pushes down on us and from every side as well. We have about fourteen pounds (6.3 kg) of air pressure pushing down on every square inch of our bodies at every moment.

What we call a vacuum is really just lower-than-normal air pressure. When you suck on a drinking straw, you are lowering the air pressure inside the straw. Then the normal pressure outside pushes the liquid up into the straw.

Air presses from all sides. So, when something like a kite or an airplane is up in the air, air pressure is pushing up and from all sides as well as pushing down from above.

The things that happen because of air speed and pressure are what make the following experiments work.

The Impossible Fluttering Paper

Do you have enough lung power to make a paper flutter that is hidden behind a bottle?

You need:

a strip of paper 4 by ½ inches (10 cm × 1.25 cm)

a large bottle
2 inches (5 cm) of tape
scissors

What to do:

Cut a strip of notebook paper four inches long and half an inch wide (10 cm × 1.25 cm). Fold the paper half an inch from the end so it looks like this:

Place the strip of tape over the folded end and tape the paper onto a tabletop so it looks like the illustration below.

Set a large bottle on the table between you and the paper. Place the bottle about three inches in front of the paper strip and blow directly at the bottle in front of you. Keep your eye on the paper strip as you blow hard, soft, fast, and slow.

What happens:
When you blow just hard enough, the paper will begin to bend and flutter even though you are blowing on the bottle instead of the paper.

Why:
Moving air will follow a curved surface. It does not always travel in a straight line the way light rays do. Even though your breath of air is deflected when it strikes the bottle, some of the air continues around the bottle, striking the paper strip.

What now:
See how far away from the bottle you can blow and still make the paper flutter. Move the paper closer to the bottle or farther away and check your results. Just remember to rest a minute between blowing efforts so you don't get dizzy.

The Stubborn Ping-Pong Ball

Anyone can blow a Ping-Pong ball a few inches. Or can they?

You need:

a large funnel
a Ping-Pong ball

a sheet of paper and tape
(if you don't have a funnel)

What to do:

Wash the funnel carefully to make certain it is absolutely clean. A funnel used around the kitchen is the only kind to use for this experiment. Don't use a funnel that has been used around oil and gasoline in the garage.

If you don't have a funnel, it takes about ten seconds to make a paper cone. Roll a sheet of notebook paper into a cone that is large at one end and a quarter of an inch (6 mm) across at the other. Tape the loose end so your cone looks like this:

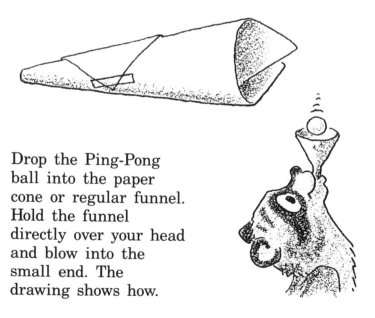

Drop the Ping-Pong ball into the paper cone or regular funnel. Hold the funnel directly over your head and blow into the small end. The drawing shows how.

The object is to blow the ball out of the funnel. Blow hard but blow steadily.

What happens:
Unless you are using a very small funnel, you'll find it is impossible to blow the ball out of it.

Why:
The passage of air around the ball makes it jump and bounce but *not* fly out of the funnel. This is because the fast-moving air flows around the ball instead of pushing it upwards. The ball tends to jump up (even higher at times than the rim of the funnel) but it won't jump to one side.

Puzzling Paper Loop

Here's a paper loop that does just the opposite of what you'd expect it to do.

You need:
a sheet of notebook
  paper
scissors

a drinking straw
tape or glue

What to do:
Cut a strip from the notebook paper about eight inches (20 cm) long and one and a half inches (3.75 cm) wide. Glue or tape the loose ends together to form a circular loop like this:

The next step calls for a drinking straw. If you don't have one, just roll a hollow tube from half a sheet of notebook paper.

Point the straw at the paper loop and blow through it. The air from the straw gives the loop a good push and the loop rolls away across the table.

Now place the loop on the table in front of you. Aim the straw so that it is above the loop, pointing to the side that's away from you at an angle, as shown in the drawing.

Now blow sharply through the straw.

What happens:

The loop will either stay where it is or roll away from you. If it doesn't roll away from you, towards the burst of air coming out of the straw, then change the angle of the straw. Blow again.

Once you have the correct angle for the straw and get the feel of exactly how hard you need to blow, you can astound friends by making the paper loop follow the air rather than run from it.

Why:

Moving air creates a low pressure area as it flows along. The paper loop is moved into that low pressure area by the normal air pressure behind it and on its sides.

The fact that moving air—or something moving through the air—creates a low pressure area is one of the things that enables airplanes to fly. Air flowing past a curved surface tends to speed up. The faster it flows the lower the pressure it creates. This tells you something about creating low pressure on top of a curved airplane to supply the "lift" the plane needs to fly.

The Great Coin and Paper Race

The outcome of this race between a coin and a piece of paper is amazing.

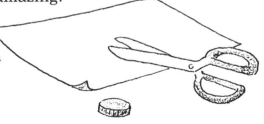

You need:
a fairly large coin
paper
scissors

What to do:
Cut a round piece of paper that is a little smaller than the coin. It doesn't have to be perfectly round, but keep it as nearly round as possible. Just be sure it doesn't stick out at any point past the edge

of the coin when you place the coin on top of the paper.

You're going to use the coin and paper in a scientific race. Hold the coin in one hand and the paper in the other about three feet (.9 m) above the floor. Drop them both at the same instant. Note what happens.

What happens:

The coin takes off for the floor in a straight line while the paper flutters this way and that and reaches the floor long afterwards. Their paths look like this:

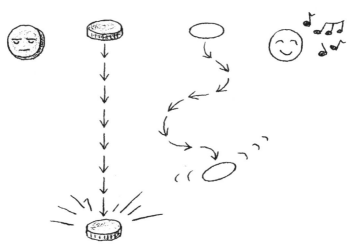

Why:

The coin is heavy enough so that its fall is not disturbed as gravity draws it down.

The paper is extremely light in weight, but it has about the same amount of surface as the coin. This combination of lots of surface plus light weight causes the paper to flutter because the air pushes at it as it falls.

114

The Great Coin and Paper Race— *Second Stage*

It's only fair to let the loser in any race have a second shot at winning.

You need:
the coin and paper from the previous experiment

What to do:
Hold the paper and the coin in the same hand with the paper sitting on top of the coin. Hold them like this:

Hold the coin by its edges so you don't touch the paper at all. Drop them now.

What happens:
The coin and paper should travel together all the way to the floor. If any air gets between them they will separate and the paper will finish its journey fluttering instead of falling with the coin. If that happens, repeat the experiment.

Why:
The paper and the coin travel together because of moving air. When something moves rapidly through the air (such as the falling coin), it pulls some air immediately behind it.

The paper "rides" the coin down because it is caught in the pocket of air travelling with the speeding coin.

The Great Coin Blowing Demonstration

Do you know anyone who can blow hard enough to blow a small coin all the way across the mouth of a glass? Of course you do. You can!

You need:
a glass   a small coin

What to do:
Balance a small coin on the rim of a drinking glass like this:

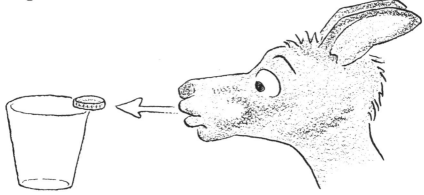

Blow sharply on the edge of the coin. The arrow in the drawing shows where to direct the stream of air.

Now, balance the coin on the rim of the glass again. This time you are going to blow the coin all the way across the open mouth of the glass so that it lands on the table or desk on the opposite side of the glass.

Impossible? No. You can do it!

Give a hard blow. Most likely the coin will fall into the glass. (That's what happened to me the first three times I tried it.)

You must blow right at the edge of the coin. Check the arrow in the illustration again. Don't blow over the coin and don't blow under it. Don't place your lips too close to the coin. Stay back several inches and blow straight at the coin's edge. Blow hard and fast.

What happens:
The first time you tried it, the coin fell off the rim of the glass. It may have fallen into the glass or onto the table. But that's what you expected, wasn't it?

When you lined up everything correctly, the coin sailed across the glass and landed on the other side. It might have hit the opposite rim, but the force of the rapidly moving air kept it going.

Why:
The coin is light enough for the moving air from your lungs to set it in motion. It had very little friction to overcome, because the coin was balanced delicately on the rim of the glass.

It's all a matter of directing the coin in the path it needs to take. Air speed docs the rest.

What's the Matter With This Bottle?

Here's a bottle of water with an open top, but you can't empty it.

You need:

a 2- or 3-liter plastic
soft drink bottle
sticky cloth or plastic
tape

a large pitcher of
water
a funnel

What to do:

Place the funnel in the mouth of the bottle. Carefully and tightly seal the funnel onto the bottle as seen here:

Use very sticky black cloth or plastic tape such as friction tape or electrician's tape. Grey duck tape will work, but you'll have to tear the wide tape into strips that are about half an inch (1.25 cm) wide.

Take your time and work with strips of tape eight or ten inches (10 or 12.5 cm) long. Make certain you tape the funnel onto the bottle so the seal is airtight. Pull the tape tight and press it down firmly.

Set the bottle and funnel in the sink. Fill a pitcher with water and start filling the bottle. But wait a minute! Be sure you pour water into the funnel fast enough so the water level rises in the funnel. This is extremely important! Keep pouring so the water level is near the top of the funnel.

Now, place your hand tightly over the top of the funnel (which is full of water) and quickly turn the bottle over so it looks like this:

Keep your hand over the mouth of the funnel until the air inside the bottle rises into what is actually the bottom of the bottle. Don't let even a tiny bubble of air get past your hand into the mouth of the funnel.

What happens:
The water stays in the bottle.

Why:
With the space between the funnel and bottle taped airtight and the funnel full of water, air is

trapped inside the bottle with no way to escape. As water fills the bottle the air molecules inside are pressed more and more tightly together.

Eventually, the air molecules are so compressed that the air pressure inside the bottle is equal to the pressure of the water pushing against it.

So long as not even a bubble of extra air works its way into the bottle, the air pressure on the outside will hold the water in the bottle.

A Person Could Die of Thirst

What could be more annoying than to stick a drinking straw into a bottle and then find it impossible to suck any of the liquid up into your mouth.

You need:

a soda bottle nearly
full of water

a drinking straw
a roll of sticky tape

What to do:

Fill a soda bottle nearly full of water. Place a drinking straw in the bottle.

Pull off a strip of sticky cloth or plastic tape about eight inches (10 cm) long. Wrap it carefully and tightly around the mouth of the bottle so it forms an airtight seal around the straw. Use a second and maybe even a third strip of tape to make sure no air can get through the seal.

Place your mouth on the end of the straw and begin to suck on it as you normally would. Don't take your mouth away from the straw after you begin trying to drink through it.

What happens:
You won't get more than just a tiny bit of water out of the straw, if you get anything at all.

Why:
Early in this chapter we mentioned that it is the outside air pressure that enables us to drink through a straw. Unless air can push down on the liquid in a glass or bottle, it is impossible to drink through a straw.

As you suck on the straw you lower the air pressure inside the straw. Outside pressure normally pushes the liquid up into the straw. But, since you sealed the top of the bottle shut, the outside air can't push on the water in the bottle, and you're out of luck when it comes to drinking through that straw.

The Paper Wad That Won't Go Into the Bottle

No great effort is required to put a small wad of paper into a bottle. So why won't this paper wad do what you ask it to do?

You need:

a small mouthed bottle

a piece of scrap paper

What to do:

Place the bottle on its side on the table.

Wad a small piece of paper into a ball about the size of a green pea. Then place the paper wad in the bottle's mouth as seen here.

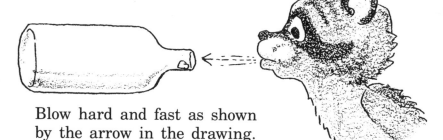

Blow hard and fast as shown by the arrow in the drawing.

What happens:

Instead of flying into the bottle the paper wad is more likely to fly out of the bottle's mouth and come back toward you.

Why:

The fast-moving air goes past the paper wad and strikes the bottom of the bottle. This increases the air pressure inside the bottle. As that compressed air rushes out, it carries the paper wad out with it.

How to Empty a Glass By Blowing On It

It's easy to empty a glass by pouring the water from it. But it's more fun to blow on it to accomplish the same thing.

You need:

2 glasses the same size   a drinking straw
a bowl or pan   water

What to do:

Run enough water into the sink so the water level is a little higher than the width of the glasses when they are turned on their sides. Here's how:

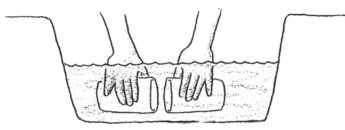

Make sure the glasses are full of water. Press the two rims together. Get a firm hold on both glasses and lift them out of the sink with their rims still pressed together.

Now turn them a quarter turn so that one glass is on top of the other as shown on page 124.

Be sure to set the two glasses in an empty bowl or pan. This is really important.

It's also important that you don't let the wet glasses slip out of your hands!

Very carefully slide the top glass a bit to one side

so the rims of the glass no longer meet exactly. Do this slowly and no water will run out of the top glass. Here's how the glasses look in relation to each other:

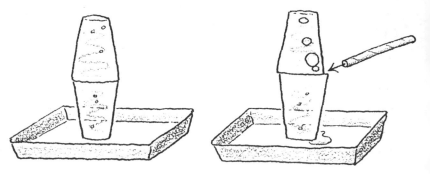

Aim the drinking straw right at the point shown by the arrow where there is a tiny space between the rims of the glasses. Now blow gently through the straw. Then blow a bit harder.

What happens:
Air bubbles will rise inside the top glass and a stream of water will flow down the side of the bottom glass into the container. Within a short time the top glass will be totally empty.

Why:
Air pressure outside the glasses combines with surface tension to keep the water in the top glass from running out and into the container when you move their rims apart slightly.

When you blow, the air pressure from the end of the straw overcomes the water's surface tension and forces air between the two glasses. Once inside the glasses, the air rises since it is lighter than water.

A Great Experiment or a Wet Trick

Try this as a great science experiment. Then decide whether to use it as a wet trick.

You need:

a plastic bottle (soft drink or dish soap kind)

pliers

a small nail

water

What to do:

Begin by making a dozen or so very small holes in the bottom of the bottle. A small nail is all you need for this. Hold the nail in the pliers and use the pliers to push the nail's point into the bottle's bottom.

Once you've made a dozen of so little holes, set the bottle in the sink. Run a couple of inches (5 cm) of water into the sink so the water rises well above the holes you just made. Hold onto the bottle to keep it from floating and tipping onto its side.

Now fill the bottle to the top with water. The water in the sink keeps the water you pour in from coming out the holes in the bottom. Lift the bottle above the water in the sink for a second to make sure water comes out the holes.

Once the bottle is totally full, screw on the cap and slowly lift the bottle up above the water in the sink.

What happens:

A few droplets may form around the holes but the bottle will not leak.

While you're still holding the bottle over the sink, remove the cap and the water will flow out through the holes you punched. Your experiment looks like this:

Why:

So long as no water can push down through the open mouth of the bottle, the outside air pressure holds the water inside the tiny holes. Once you open the cap, air pressure pushes down through the bottle's mouth and out the water comes.

What now:

You can use this as an outdoor practical joke. Pretend you can't open the cap, which you have screwed on fairly tight. Ask someone to help. Of course, that person will be able to open the lid and maybe even laugh at you for being so weak.

But when the lid loosens, whoever is holding the bottle is going to get wet.

INDEX